When I coul
and his wife
for the first

thoughts on the subject. As I wrote, I came to the
conclusion that the greatest gift we can give our
grandkids is to pray for them. May this book inspire
each reader to be…

A Praying Grandparent

The best gift a child can have

By Dorothy Hsu Seitzinger

PRESS

"Grandchildren are the crowning glory of the aged."
Proverbs 17:6

Dedication

To my children who made me a grandma

To my grandchildren who have increased my
capacity to love

To my husband who loves me unconditionally

And to my brother, Luther, and his wife, Sharon,
whose grandchild, Grant, was the inspiration
for this book

INTRODUCTION

Praying for Grandchildren

My prayers for my grandchildren began long before they were born. In fact, on both of my daughters' wedding days just before walking down the aisle, I prayed with them. I held their hands in mine and asked God to bless their marriages. I prayed that the blessing would include children. After years of marriage, however, my girls remained childless, and it appeared that God was answering my prayer "no." But I didn't stop praying. At times I even fasted as I beseeched God for my daughters.

And when God finally **did** answer "yes," it was different from what I expected. "We're thinking of adopting," my older daughter told me. And immediately I began to pray for the little one that God had planned for them. We thought it would be a girl. But we were surprised again. When they saw the face of the little boy in a Russian orphanage they knew he was the one. And in a few months they had returned with my first grandchild. I had known in my **head** that I could love an adopted grandchild, but when

I held Paul Min in my arms for the first time, my heart nearly burst. All of us in the airport began to sing "Praise God From Whom All Blessings Flow." He was our precious, precious gift. I had the same reaction two years later when we welcomed a little granddaughter, Lia, from China. And in a few more years, the Lord surprised my other daughter with two miraculous pregnancies and Micah and Jessie were born.

To add to the surprises during those years was my marriage to a dear man (widowed like I was) who was blessed with 5 granddaughters, Lindsay, Sarah, Stefi, Lauren, and Raeal, and a great grandson, Kole. And so we were given 10 grandchildren to love, 10 grandchildren to pray for (and more are on the way). And we lift them to our Father every day.

Now That I Am One

I used to think that
No one
Could pray for a child
More earnestly than a
Parent.
I've changed my mind.
Now that I am one,
I believe it's a
Grandparent.

Perfectly Formed

Protect my grandchild
Growing in my daughter.
I don't know yet whether
He's a he,
Or a she.
But You do.
Cause his tiny lungs and arms
And brain to grow perfectly.
Keep his heart beating
Strong.
But Lord,
When he's born,
If he doesn't seem perfect in
Our eyes,
We'll love him still.
For we know he's perfect in
Yours.

Like Himself

When I held my newborn
Grandson for the first
Time
I studied him intently.
I examined his
Eyes,
His mouth,
His ears,
Every tiny detail of his
Face
Looking for some resemblance.
I wanted him to look like my
Daughter,
A sense of family
Pride.
But as hard as I searched
I couldn't find a single trait
I recognized.
Maybe one day I'll be able to say
"He's got his mommy's
Eyes or hair."
But right now,
He simply looks like
Himself.

A New Kind of Love

How could I love my child's
Child
So intensely?
At my age
I thought I knew all about
Love.
But I was wrong.
I discovered a new kind of
Love
When I became a
Grandma.

On the Sidelines

We saw our grandson roll
Over for the very first
Time.
It was quite an event.
We all hollered.
We cheered.
We clapped.
We urged him to do it
Again.
We will always cheer their
Accomplishments,
Whether large or small.
We won't always be there to see them
Though.
So I'm glad we saw our
Grandson
Roll over for the first time
Today.

Perspective

A parent looks ahead
And wonders how long the
Sleepless nights and
Stressful days
Will last.
A grandparent looks back
And wonders how those
Days
Could have gone by so
Fast.

Remind Me

Lord,
I prayed for grandchildren for a long
Time.
It took years for You to
Answer.
But finally, they
Came,
Some adopted
And some not.
Remind me which is
Which.

Big and Little

When our grandkids are
Small
We tell their parents,
"Little children,
Little problems.
Big children,
Big problems."
That adage may be true.
But to my kids right now,
The little problems
Seem really
Big.

Wake-Up Call

Something woke us.
We were spending the night at
Our daughter's house
When we felt a
Movement in the
Bed.
Was it the dog?
No.
It was our daughter placing
Our three-month-old
Grandson
Between us in bed.
We were suddenly wide awake.
We tickled him till
He broke out into that
Smile
That makes us melt.
Soon Mommy cradled him in her arms
And left.
And we were left with the memory
Of waking up
And finding our grandson in our
Bed.

A Lingering Gift

Grandma had left on the
Plane
And her grandson, Matthew,
Was missing her.
He crawled into the bed
Where she had
Slept.
"Mommy, Mommy, come here,"
He shouted.
"Grandma left something."
Mommy came, expecting to find
One of her mother's special
Rings.
"No, Mommy, can't you tell?
Grandma left her pretty smell."

Moving

My grandchildren
Moved,
Not just across town,
But across the state.
It wasn't supposed to happen,
Lord.
I prayed their daddy would find
A job here,
Not in Cleveland.
I want them to still come
To supper on Tuesday nights.
I want to sit with them
In church.
I want to see them come
Running out to the car to give me a hug
When I stop by.
My grandchildren moved, Lord,
And I hurt.
But I'm glad distance can't
Affect my love
Or my prayers.
(And I'm glad Cleveland
Isn't in California.)

Every Single Day

Every single day
We pray.
For:
Paul Min,
Lia,
Sarah,
Stefi,
Micah,
Jessie,
Lindsay,
Kole,
Lauren and
Raeal.
Every single day
We pray.

Is He Still Praying?

I know a grandpa
Who prayed for his grandchildren
Everyday.
Two did great.
They're serving you, Lord.
Two strayed,
Terribly.
They are still so very far
Away.
The grandpa died.
He's with You.
Is he still praying for them,
Lord?

Bickering

The bickering bothers me,
Lord.
He teases her.
She cries.
I try to be their peacemaker.
I know they love each
Other,
But it doesn't always show.
I used to fight with my brothers
Too.
But now that we're older
We're really good
Friends.
Help me remember that,
Lord.
Especially today.

Grandmother Lois

Paul loved Timothy like a son.
He knew his grandmother
Too.
Paul said her name was Lois
And that she had great
Faith.
Paul prayed much for
Timothy.
But I suspect that Lois
Prayed even
More.

Long-Ago Prayers

We knew when we went to
Grandma and Grandpa
Combs' house
That we would have
Devotions.
They would always pray
Loooooooooooong
Prayers.
My girls got fidgety.
But they listened.
They're grown
Now
With children of their own.
And they can't think of
Grandma and Grandpa Combs
Without remembering
Those prayers.
They didn't really appreciate them
Then,
But they do now.

Protect Them

Protect them today,
Lord.
Danger lurks:
Germs,
Speeding cars,
Pornography,
Deception.
I don't know what they'll face
Today,
But You do, Lord.
Protect them.

You Knew

They already know he's
A boy
And she still has
Five months to go.
But that's nothing.
You knew him, Lord,
Before his parents
Were even
Born.

Remind Us

We're a little worried, Lord
He's still not
Talking.
Remind us of our concern
In a few years
When he won't be
Quiet.

The Best Gift

We couldn't wait for him to
Open his birthday gift
Today.
It was a B. B. gun,
A genuine Daisy Red Ryder.
Grandpa thinks every boy needs
One.
I'm not so sure.
But one thing I am sure
About.
The best gift a child can have
Is a praying
Grandparent.

Snail Mail

I'm glad in this age of
Cell phones
And
Electronic mail
That we still get
Hand scrawled notes
In the mail box
Like the one we got
Today:

Dear Grandma and grandpa,

Thank you for
the BBgun.
Love,
Paul Min

The Last to Give Up

My friend's grandson is in
Prison.
Everyone else has given up
On him,
But not my friend.
It seems to me, Lord,
That a grandparent
Is the last to give up,
Except for You.

The Greatest Prayer

I asked the Lord,
"What's the greatest prayer
I can ever pray for my
Grandchild?"
He said,
"Pray that he will love Me
With all his heart,
Soul, mind, and strength
And his neighbor as himself.
And while you're at it,
Pray the same prayer for
Yourself."

Estrangement

They're estranged.
My friend's son left the state
With his family.
He broke off all
Communication.
It's been years now.
Why?
Only he knows.
He's robbing himself.
But most sadly,
He's robbing his
Children
Of ever knowing their
Grandparents.
But Lord,
I'm certain that
He can never, ever
Rob them,
Of their grandparents'
Prayers.

Real Trouble

When my husband speaks to
Teenagers
He likes to say,
"You're in real
Trouble
If you have a praying
Grandma."

Too Early?

My grandson's only two, Lord.
Is it too early
To pray for the woman who will
One day be his
Wife?

You'd better get
Started.
Her grandparents
Are already praying for
Him.

Her Teacher

It happened to her grandpa
And me.
May it happen again
Today, Lord.
When my granddaughter
Meets her teacher for the
First time,
May it be love at first
Sight.

Art Galleries

I've been to the art gallery in
Columbus,
Cincinnati, and even
Chicago.
But I've seen nothing
That compares to the art
Gallery on my
Refrigerator.

I Samuel 12:23

I changed just one of Samuel's
Words
To make them mine:
"God forbid that I should
Sin against the
Lord
In ceasing to pray for my
Grandchildren." (KJV)

Our Song

I don't know when the song first became "ours," for it was a familiar one that we had sung for years. Actually, it's a Bible verse set to music. Psalm 118:24: "This is the day that the Lord has made. We will rejoice and be glad in it." I had sung it with my preschoolers when I was a teacher; and when my new husband and I were married, we began singing it on our way to church on Sunday mornings. And then we began to sing it each morning after our devotional time together. And finally, we began calling it "our song."

It is more than a catchy tune, although we have added a few fun flourishes to it. It gets our hearts in the right frame of mind at the beginning of the day. The verse points out that the Lord has **made** the day. He knows what it will hold. And it affirms that we can choose to rejoice no matter what surprises the day may bring.

We've taught the song to our grandkids, too. When they spend the night, we gather them close and greet the morning with our exuberant melody. For our out-of-town grandkids we use the phone. We call them once a week or so, and when they hear our voices, they know what to expect, and they join in singing, too. Our eight-year-old grandson even taught himself to play the tune on the piano.

And we sang it to our newest grandson before he was even born. Putting our mouths close to his mom's big belly, we belted out the words. Now, although he is still too young to sing it with us, he can listen. Just recently, when he picked up the phone, his mommy asked, "Do you want Grandmomma and Pop Pop to sing to you?" "Ya," he said. So she called us, and we joyfully sang our song to him. We could picture his smile as he held his ear to the telephone.

Sometimes we almost shout out the words in the morning. We're excited to greet the day. On other mornings it takes a lot of effort to even form the words. Our bodies may be aching or our hearts breaking. But we sing it anyway, because it's true. We hope it will be true for our grandkids, too. We hope they will never outgrow our song. We hope that **our** song will become **theirs.**

A Grandparent's Heart

The love I felt for my first grandchild
Was so intense
I wondered when the second was
On the way,
"Can I possibly love this next child
As much?"
I needn't have worried.
For each grandchild has increased
My capacity to love.
I've discovered that a grandparent's
Heart
Always has room for one
More.

Jesiah

The Answers

They're first time
Parents, Lord,
And we're old
Timers.
We think we know all the
Answers,
But we don't.

How Do I Pray?

I'm upset.
I'm distraught.
I see her headed for
Disaster.
What do I do?
How do I pray, Lord?

Sometimes the only
Thing you can do
Is cry,
"Help!"

Helping in Sunday School

She's 12 now, and
Acting so grown up.
"Why not help us in
Sunday school,
We suggested.
"Sure,"
Was her reply.
Today was her first day.
She put out the snack for the
Three-year-olds.
She read Anah a
Story.
She wiped up spills.
She was responsible.
We've been praying that
She will follow you
Lord.
Thanks for letting us
Help.

Names

They call us Grandma and
Grandpa,
Or Grandmomma and
Pop Pop,
Or sometimes just
Granny.
But we really don't care
What they call us.
Each name means
Love.

Help Me

Lord,
Help me be as good
As my grandchild
Thinks I am.

Babysitting

After babysitting
Our two-year-old grandson
For a week
I've intensified my
Prayers,
Not for him
But for his parents.

Micah

Something's Wrong

The grandma knew early on
That something was
Wrong.
He didn't develop like the
Others.
He couldn't respond.
He was in his own perplexing
World.
Was it autism?
Perhaps.
The diagnosis still isn't
Clear.
But it is clear that the grandma
Loves this child like the rest.
Oh, how she loves him,
And prays for the
Best.
But it's also clear
That there are some problems
Even love can't
Fix.

Saying Yes

Her familiar little voice was on the
Phone.
"Grandma,
Can I come and spend the
Night?"
There were other things to do.
But I said,
"Sure, we'll have a great time."
And we did.
Whenever it's possible,
A grandma says,
"Yes."

Saying No

Her daughter moved back home
With her four kids.
She says,
"Bye, Mom. I'm meeting
My friends."
Grandma watches the kids,
Cooks,
Cleans,
And pays the bills.
Grandpa hides out in his
Study.
Sometimes even a grandma
Should say,
"No."

Grandparent's Day

It was Grandparent's Day
In kindergarten.
I looked around at the grandparents
As we watched our grandkids
Present a little
Program.
We smiled till our faces
Hurt.
We strained to hear every
Word,
And we couldn't wait to
Clap.
Whoever thought peacocks were
Proud
Hasn't seen a grandparent on
Grandparent's Day!

Havens

Lord,
So many children live in
Broken,
Dysfunctional families.
May our homes be
Shelters for them,
Havens of
Love,
Acceptance,
And peace.
In us, Lord,
May they see
What a godly marriage
Should be.

My Neck

When I taught preschool
A four-year-old told me,
"You look like a grandma."
I waited for the rest.
"Because of your neck."
I always wanted to be a
Grandma.
But I never wanted to
Look like
One.

Stefanie

Grandma

Three Important Words

My dad was a good
Man,
A farmer who lived to be
Ninety-six.
For five of those last years
He lived with me.
I saw him sit on the edge of his
Bed
With a Bible open on his lap.
I heard him pray.
I'm sure he prayed for his
Grandchildren.
He delighted to hear of their
Accomplishments.
He saved the cards
They sent
And had me post all their pictures
On the wall.
He loved them.
But he couldn't say those words.
He had never learned how.
I doubt that his stoic, German
Mom or dad
Had ever said those words to
Him.
Maybe that's why I've told
My grandkids at least a zillion
Times,
"I love you."

The Good Years

My mom was a farmer's
Wife.
She worked hard from dawn
Till bedtime.
She loved you, Lord,
And she loved her children and
Grandchildren.
But her mind was
Fragile;
And in her older years
It failed her.
I hope my brain stays
Sharp
Till you take me home, Lord.
I try to exercise it.
I read,
Work crossword puzzles,
And play Scrabble.
But if my mind does
Deteriorate one day,
Lord.
Let my grandkids remember
The good years
And not the
Bad.

Introductions

When Jack and I were
First married,
I found myself introducing the
Girls
As "**his**" grandkids.
One day Stefi told me,
"We're your granddaughters,
Too."
She was right.
Now,
I always say they're
Ours.

They'll Know

They'll know their great grandpa
Still mowed
My lawn when he was
Ninety-five.
They'll know their great grandma
Was the one who
Made the beautiful
Quilts
Displayed on their walls
And beds.
They'll know their Grandpa Hsu
Came from China and
Died when their mommies
Were small.
They'll know how God
Carried us through those
Hard,
Hard days.
They'll know how God gave
Them another grandpa
Who loves to make them
Laugh.
I will tell them.
That's how they'll know.

"But watch out! Be very careful never to forget what you have seen the Lord do for you. Do not let these things escape from your mind as long as you live! And be sure to pass them on to your children and grandchildren" Deuteronomy 4:9.

Fundraisers

So far this year we've bought
Candles
And a trivet
And wrapping paper
With bows.
We're the first ones
They ask,
And the last to say
No.

A New Granddad

I could tell he was a new
Grandpa,
Not because of the smile
Spread across his
Face,
Or the spring in his
Step.
I knew because he whipped his
Billfold out of his
Pocket and said,
"I have a few pictures."

A Call In The Night

We were sound asleep when the
Call came.
My daughter was crying.
"Pray for Micah,
He's been screaming with pain
And he's on the way to
The hospital right now."
Grandpa and I did pray.
We prayed hard.
And all night long
As I kept waking up
And felt fear grip my heart,
I prayed again:
"Protect my little grandson, Lord.
Give the doctors wisdom.
Calm his parents' hearts.
And calm mine, too."
Morning finally came.
I called as early as I could,
Wondering what I would hear.
"He's home.
He's asleep.
The tests were all normal."
And Grandpa and I prayed
Once more:
"Thank you,
Thank you,
Thank you, Lord."

Can I Help?

"Can I help?"
He asked Grandpa as he was
Getting ready to fix
Breakfast.
So Grandpa decked out our
Grandson in an oversized
Apron,
And a chef's hat
And showed him how to scramble
Eggs.
"Can I help?" she asked
As I began to water the flowers.
So I gave my granddaughter
A sprinkling can of
Her own.
"Can I help?" he asked
When Grandpa began to clean the
Fish.
So we fixed him up with a
Pair of rubber gloves,
And plunging his hands
Into the icy water
He handed fish after fish to
Grandpa.
No wonder they like to come to our
House.

Too Young to Die

His granddaughter's dying.
She's battled the disease
Since she was three,
More than twenty years ago.
Her fight has been
Brave,
Intense,
Almost more than he could bear to
Watch.
Now that her battle's coming to an
End,
He can't understand,
Nor can I,
Why you didn't take him home
First.

Unconditional Love

Their daughter isn't married,
But she's pregnant.
And she's determined to keep
The baby.
They wish they could change
Things,
But they can't.
Of one thing they are sure.
This baby will need their love as
Much as their other
Grandchildren.
No,
This baby will need their love
Even more.

Resemblance

In my eyes he's beautiful.
I love his bald
Head,
And white beard.
He looks great for
Seventy-eight.
But it scares the grandkids
When he says,
"You're looking more like me
Every day."

Fishing

When the grandkids came for
A visit,
We had only one day to
Take them fishing.
And it looked like rain.
But we got ready to go
Anyway.
In the car Grandpa prayed
That the rain wouldn't stop us.
(He added that 12 fish
Would be enough for
Supper.)
It was wet at the
Pond,
But the rain held off
For an hour and a half.
When we headed for
Home,
We counted the fish.
There were
12.

Trouble in School

He got in trouble at school today.
I was troubled, too.
I wanted to fix things, right
Now.
Grandpa calmed me down.
He told me about the time
He set a fire
On the porch
And lied about it.
He told about slipping his hand
Under Grandma's pillow
And stealing money
From her coin purse.
He told me about using his fists
On kids.
"And look at me now," he said.
His words helped.
But I still wish he hadn't gotten
In trouble at school
Today.

Our Time

"Take us to the pool, Grandma.
And will you play
Tea party with me?
Just one more book,
And another game of
Uno, too.
One more of your funny
Stories, Grandpa.
Just one more."
More than our Christmas gifts
And the dollars we slip in their
Cards.
They just want our
Time.
(Grandpa added:
At this stage of their lives.)

Recycling

I'm glad I kept the highchair,
The "jammies,"
And the baby spoons.
I'm glad I didn't give away
The books,
The puzzles,
And the Fisher Price toys.
But I wish I'd
Had the sense
(And the space)
To keep
More.

Paid Up

The elderly lady had
Already paid her
Dues.
She confided to my
Friend,
"The best part about being a
A great grandma is
They don't ask you to babysit
Anymore."

I Like To Ask

I like to ask her:
"If all the five-year-old girls
In the whole world
Were lined up
In one long line,
Who would I pick to be my
Granddaughter?
And she likes to answer,
"Me!"

Across the Miles

My friend kept her grandkids
For awhile.
She had hoped they could stay
Longer,
But her health
Gave out.
Their mother is incapable,
So they are now in foster
Homes
Far across the country.
But my friend
Writes,
Calls,
Sends gifts,
Visits,
Pleads their case with the
Authorities, and
Prays.
She's their grandma,
She loves them.
And she won't let them
Forget.

*God is answering her prayers. Two of her grandchildren have now been adopted by a loving Christian couple.

A Day to Remember

The first sign of trouble was the
Water dripping
Through the kitchen ceiling.
It took just seconds to find the
Problem.
A three-year-old
And a six-year-old
Had turned on the faucets in the
Bathroom overhead.
But first,
They had stuffed the drains with
Lots of toilet paper,
Lots of it.
They had stuffed the toilet,
Too.
Both blamed the other.
But both got punished.
And both had to help clean up the
Mess.
It's a day the parents will
Remember,
But one the kids would like to
Forget.

I've Got One Now!

In kindergarten
They were discussing how
The children got their
Names.
Paul Min said he was named
After his grandfathers.
The teacher added,
"They're both in heaven,
Aren't they?"
Paul Min nodded.
But he wasn't finished with
The topic of grandpas.
Thinking about the man I
Recently married,
He proudly proclaimed,
"But I've got one now!"

The Treasure

The gift is obviously
Homemade
With lots of glittery
Spangles and
Glue.
It's one that only a grandma
Would treasure.
(And put out for
Display.)

The Recipe

At family dinners we could
Always count on
One dish being there.
It was my mom's specialty:
Baked noodles.
I don't know where she got the
Recipe, for it was written only in her
Head.
But she taught me to make it,
To take little bites
Till it tasted exactly
Right.
I coached my daughter
Till she learned the process, too.
And now, in her e-mails she
Often says,
"I made Grandma's Noodles
Today."
(That's the name we call it now.)
It won't ever be exactly like
Grandma's
For her noodles were homemade.
But it's close enough.
I hope my daughter teaches
Her daughter who
Will teach her daughter, too.
Most of mom's recipes died with
Her,
But I hope this one
Survives.

Grandma Seventrit

No one is more convinced than my husband of the effectiveness of a grandparent's prayers. He loves to share the story of his Grandma Seventrit.

I was only six years old when Grandma came to live with us. My mother had died; and when my dad remarried a beautiful young wife, her mother came along as part of the bargain. I never called her step-grandma. She was my real grandma through and through. Since there weren't enough bedrooms in the house, Grandma and I shared one. Her bed was on one side, mine on the other, with just a night stand between us. I didn't mind sharing a room with her; for I had a fear of the dark, and it was nice to have company. We shared that room till I was 12 years old.

Grandma had arthritis, and she taught me to brush and braid her long hair. It became a bedtime routine; and as I drifted off to sleep I was aware of her loving presence in the room. I became aware, too, of her prayers. I remember waking during the night and hearing her beseeching the Lord in her thick German accent. I couldn't understand all she said, but I heard her call out the names of Howard and Betty (my dad and stepmother). And I know she prayed for me and my two brothers, too. We all needed prayer, for my dad was a devout heathen, a profane man who said after my mother had died, "There is no God." My stepmom was a nominal churchgoer, and my brothers and I knew nothing about salvation. I also had a strong fear of death.

One morning I saw the result of my grandma's prayers. My dad and stepmom had unknowingly stumbled onto a Bible study the night before and were persuaded to stay. Before they left at 4:00 in the morning, they had both given their lives to Jesus. Overnight they were changed. Dad became an outgoing witness for the Lord. As he shared what he had learned, I accepted Christ into my life, too. Our house became a loving home.

Even though Grandma's heart was weak physically (she spent most of her latter years in bed), spiritually she was strong. She showed me what it meant to love and trust God with a whole heart. And God continued to answer her prayers even after she was gone. For it was then that my two brothers came to the Lord, too. Grandma was my buddy. Grandma was my encourager. But most of all, Grandma was my prayer warrior.

(And Grandma's heart proved to be stronger than we thought. When she was 65, her doctor told us she wouldn't last the night. Two years later, the doctor died, and Grandma lived on to be 93.)

Earning Respect

We went along to school
Today
To celebrate our grandson's
Birthday.
He was eight.
He was also the "star."
He read a story to the whole
Class,
Displayed pictures,
And passed out cookies.
And he answered questions.
When the teacher asked
Who he most respected,
He said,
"Grandma and Grandpa."
May it always be true.

Gotcha Day!

"Happy Gotcha Day, Lia!"
"Happy Gotcha Day, Paul Min!"
It's a greeting we exclaim each
Year.
It's a day to party,
Like a birthday,
But even better.
It's like Thanksgiving and
Christmas combined.
For us, it's just about the
Happiest
Day of all.
For it's the day we celebrate
The official saying,
"This child now belongs to
You."

One Day

They love to be seen with us
Now,
At school,
In the park,
At McDonalds.
But if one day
They prefer to be seen
Alone,
Help us to understand.

The Walk

When you take a walk with
A two-year-old,
You go slow.
You stop and examine a leaf here,
A twig over there.
You pick up a seed pod and shake it.
You break it open
To find the seeds hidden inside.
You see the discarded plastic
Spoon too late,
And he has already put it in
His mouth
Before you can grab it.
You say, "Dirty spoon,"
And let him throw it in the
Trash can.
You pause when he points at the
Plane overhead.
And when he hears the train
A mile away,
He says, "Whoo! Whoo!"
As he pulls the pretend whistle
With his hand.
When you take a walk with a
Two-year-old,
You see the world through his
Eyes,
And you realize how much
You usually
Miss.

The Truth

Grandpa asked our
Granddaughter,
"How did you get so
Pretty?"
Before she could even
Answer
Her brother blurted out,
"God made her that
Way!"
I'm glad he's been taught
The truth.

Already Home

They had just told their
Families the good
News.
They were as excited as
Only expectant
Parents can be.
But soon their joy turned to
Horror.
The doctor informed them
Their baby,
Their very first child
Was gone.
But You saw it differently, Lord.
You saw a child coming
Home.

How Did She Do It?

I was looking at my daughter's
Library
And wondered how my
Mom
Raised six kids without
Dr. Dobson.

I Wish

My husband told me today:
"I wish I had been as
Smart when I was just a
Dad
As I am now that I'm a
Grandpa."

A Morning Prayer

Lord,
Help them adhere
To what is good
Today.
Help them flee from
Evil.
And give them a God
Sense
All day long.
Amen.

Never Getting Tired

I never get tired of hearing
Him say,
"I love you, Grandma."
I hope he never gets
Tired of
Saying it.

Job Description

Lord,
They told us the news
Tonight.
"We're pregnant again."
And we're thrilled,
But worried, too.
The timing isn't
Good.
Finances are already tight.
How will they possibly
Manage, Lord?
How?

Did you forget?
*It's **My** job to manage*
Things.
It's your job to
Trust.

His Other Grandma

I wish she could stay home.
But right now,
My daughter needs to
Work.
Each morning she takes our
Grandson
To his other grandma who lives
Nearby.
She loves him like we do.
We pray for her.
And we say,
"Thank you, Lord, for his other
Grandma."

Biting My Tongue

What a grandparent wants to say:
"You need to let him cry."
"Are you still nursing her?"
"He's too old for a pacifier."
"You let her sleep in **your** bed?"
"McDonald's again?"
"Isn't he potty trained yet?"
"He needs a time out."
What a wise grandparent says:
Nothing.

Saying Good-bye

It was hard to say good-bye
Today.
One more hug.
One more kiss.
One more glimpse of them
Standing at the
Door.
May we always leave with them
Wishing we had stayed
Longer.

Finding The Time

My friend has twenty-eight
Grandchildren,
Twenty-eight!
How can she possibly
Pray for them
Everyday?
How can she possibly
Not?

Adversity

I know you develop faith,
And perseverance,
And compassion through
Suffering, Lord.
You did it in my life
When my husband
Died.
But now,
When I see my grandchildren facing
Affliction, Lord, I plead
"Please can't there be another
Way?"

Changing Roles

"Hold my hand,
Micah,"
I say to my three-year-old
Grandson
As we cross the parking lot at
Walmart.
My mind fast forwards.
I picture a tall young man
Crossing the same
Parking lot steadying an
Elderly lady.
"Hold my hand,
Grandma."

Aching

Father,
I ache for my friends
Who can't have
Grandkids.

Daughter,
I ache for them,
Too.

Slip of the Lip

My friend had invited
Her daughter's family
To dinner.
She had prepared a new lo-cal
Recipe.
"It's good, Mom,"
Her daughter had commented.
But a few days later
My friend's grandson
Looked at her and solemnly said,
"Grandma, the other day
Mommy said your chicken was good.
But on the way home in the car
She said she really didn't like it."
Oops!

Full Circle

At our daughter's house
The topic of conversation often
Centers on our grandkids'
Pottying and sleeping
Habits.
It's a bit disconcerting
To discover we are
Discussing the same
Topics
At our house,
But for ourselves.

Needing Help

Her granddaughter hates
School.
She can't read
And the other kids tease
Her.
She has no friends.
Her grandma hurts for her,
Like only a grandma
Can.
But she can't help her.
Please, Lord,
Will You?

Comprehension

Lord, my friend's grandson
Was killed today.
He was a soldier,
A handsome
Marine,
Only 22 years old.
And he was an only
Child.
Lord,
I can't comprehend such pain.

I can.

Curly Hands

Walking down the hallway at
School,
A preschooler looked at my
Hands with their
Bulging veins, and asked,
"Why are they so
Curly?"
Now I know.
So my little granddaughter
Can play with them
While riding in the
Car.

Pay Back

I used to tell my kids,
"I hope one day you'll
Have a child who is
Acting just like
You."
Today my wish came
True.

Fatalities

I know we learn from our mistakes,
Lord.
But will You please keep
Them from making
Fatal ones?

Great Grandparenting

I can't believe our granddaughter's
Pregnant, Lord.
We're going to be
Great grandparents.
Help Rich and Linny
Be good parents,
Lord.
And help us pray just as
Intensely
For this grandchild as our
First.

Kole

Namesake

Our grandson is named for
His grandpas who are
Already in
Heaven.
He's never met them.
But when he does, one day,
May each one hold up his hand and
Exclaim,
"Give me five, Paul Min!
You made me proud
To share my name."

Tables Turned

I told the Lord:
"I don't approve of
Everything
My grandchild does."
He told me:
"Nor I, you."

Watching

Our grandkids are always
Watching us,
Lord.
And what they see
Sometimes speaks louder
Than what they
Hear.

Answered Prayer

I had prayed this day would
Come,
But I wasn't aware, at first,
That it had arrived.
I had been talking to my
Granddaughter on the
Phone.
I smiled as I listened to
Her sweet, soft
Voice.
"I prayed to God,"
She told me.
"Oh, what did you pray?"
"I asked Jesus into my heart."
The bells and whistles started
Going off in my
Brain.
"That's wonderful!" I exclaimed.
"That's the best news!
I'm so happy!"
God's Word says the angels
Rejoice
When a sinner repents.
But could their rejoicing
Possibly be as great as a
Grandma's?

Spring Break

Our granddaughter left
Today
For Washington, D.C.
She's on spring break
With four other college
Girls.
It's not a big trip, really,
Just a seven hour drive.
But they seem so young
And vulnerable.
They just see the
Adventure.
But I see the
Wild drivers,
The predators,
The pick pockets,
The crazed gun men.
Keep them safe, Lord,
And keep me
Sane.

Perseverance

She's scared, Lord.
After years of study
Our granddaughter is almost
Finished.
But the oral exams are
Demanding.
The dissertation is
Daunting.
And she's almost ill, Lord,
Afraid of failure.
Calm her heart.
Refresh her body and
Brain.
And show her that the only
Way
She could fail now
Is to give up.

More Than A Hobby

The garage has become a
Workshop.
The cars are forlornly sitting outside
And dust wafts through the screen
Door into the kitchen.
It's because of Grandpa's
New hobby.
He's making knives:
Hunting knives,
Carving knives,
Colorful knives inset with
Turquoise and polished
Bone.
He's sold a few, but mostly he's
Making them for his kids and
Grandkids.
Each is unique.
He plans them in his head,
Sometimes at night when he can't
Sleep.
He plots them out on graph paper
And then he painstakingly grinds and sands
And glues each
Part till he's satisfied with
His creation.
One day he will give one
To each of his grandchildren.
And when he does, he will be
Giving them more than a knife.
He will be giving them part of
Himself.

My Legacy

I have one last request, Lord.
When you take me
Home,
May my prayers for my
Grandchildren
Stay behind

Printed in the United States
87878LV00002B/1-249/A